THE LENT EXPERIENCE

REVISED & EXPANDED
PARTICIPANT JOURNAL

CREATED BY ERIC FERRIS

The Lent Experience Journal, Revised & Expanded

©2023 Eric Ferris. All rights reserved.

No part of this book may be reproduced or transmitted in any form, or by any means, electronic or mechanical, included photocopying, recording or by any information storage or retrieval system, without express written permission from Eric Ferris.

ISBN: 979-8-9895898-0-7

Published by:
NarratusCreative | Narratus Press
P.O. Box 1413
Hamilton, OH 45012

Design: NarratusCreative | narratuscreative.com

Produced in the United States of America

Contents

1. The TLE Story 1
2. Using *The Lent Experience* at Your Church 5
3. Traditional? 9
4. Lent FAQs 13
5. Finding The Lent Experience Videos 19
6. Getting Ready to Start! Ash Wednesday 21
7. Challenge #1: Fasting 27
8. Challenge #2: Silence & Solitude 37
9. Challenge #3: Repentance 45
10. Challenge #4: Almsgiving 53
11. Challenge #5: Forgiveness 63
12. Challenge #6: Bible Reading 71
13. Wrapping it Up 77
14. About the Author 84
15. Contact Information 85

The TLE Story

When I was a freshman in high school, my brother invited me to go to a Christian music festival called *Fishnet*. I did not know what that was. I did not even know there was such a thing as Christian music. I just knew it would be awesome to travel in an RV with a bunch of Air Force guys. And I wanted to get to know my brother. What happened over those few days changed my life. It was not a sermon. It was not some big moment. It was the look in their eyes—thousands of people—with that look in their eyes like they knew something I did not, like they knew God on a personal level and it mattered to them in a very real, everyday kind of way.

I remember sitting on the grass while one of the bands played. A banner hung over the stage that said "Lord of All." Thousands of people all around me were sitting and smiling and enjoying the concert, but something else was going on inside me, something invisible. Even the people sitting right next to me did not know it. It felt as if I were thinking these strange thoughts, but now I know that I was praying. I finally said, *God, if what these people know is You, then I want to get to know You.*

That was it. I never even spoke the words out loud.

When I got back home to New Jersey, I looked in The Yellow Pages for the kind of church my brother was going to. (These were the B.G. days – "Before Google".) I found the closest one to my house and asked my mother if she would drive me there on Sunday. Not knowing anything about church except the Catholic Masses of my childhood, I was unsure what to expect. My family had become non-practicing Catholics, so, as I look back, I have to give my mom a lot of credit for driving me to this church. (Way to go, Mom!)

I began to learn and grow in that church. I met the youth pastor and he helped me tremendously. I got baptized. And now, thirty years later, I have spent my entire adult life serving as a pastor in the local church. Who would have imagined such a thing?

I have served as a pastor in several different varieties of Christian churches: pentecostal churches, churches with charismatic leanings, and churches with more reformed leanings… and I probably like you more if you have no idea what all of that really means. I grew up Catholic, did my undergrad studies at a pentecostal Bible college, and earned a graduate degree at the evangelical Wheaton College. Add that all up and you know what I am? Theologically confused!

OK. Not really. But it does help explain a project like *The Lent Experience*. *The Lent Experience* (TLE) is designed to help a wide variety of people participate in the amazing season of the year that leads up to Easter. There are some of us who grew up observing Lent, but may not have ever really understood the meaning behind it. There are others of us who have no idea what Lent is or why we should even care. *The Lent Experience* was designed to bridge those two worlds.

It all started as a small project in 2013 when we wondered:

THE TLE STORY

What happens when you take the best of 2,000 years of a Christian tradition, capture the heart of it and re-imagine it? Whether you're a veteran of observing Lent or a rookie who is jumping in for the first time, you can join thousands of people from all over the world for an experience that just may surprise you.

The Lent Experience is exactly that...an experience...for normal people like you and me. It's not just more teaching. It's not just more information. It's not some stuffy, religious obligation. It's an invitation to do something different because as the saying goes "If you always do what you've always done, you'll always get what you've always got". You can listen to 100 teachings about these things or you can step in and experience them for yourself in a simple, fun, and meaningful way.

Here's How it Works
You have the participant journal, so now all you need is access to the videos. The videos can be found on both RightNow Media and YouTube. Simply search "The Lent Experience" on either platform.

You watch a video on Ash Wednesday that sets up the whole thing. Then, that following Sunday and every Sunday until Easter, you watch a brief video that gives you your Lent Experience challenge for the week. You have the entire week to complete the challenge. The challenges are based on things that have been a part of Lent for centuries. Not only will you be joining thousands of people all over the world this year, but also the millions of Christians throughout the ages who have observed Lent. How cool is that?

The Lent Experience Journal

Consider this journal your guide and companion during The Lent Experience. It has helpful information, tips for accomplishing each challenge and space for you to write your thoughts and prayers. It's that easy. You simply watch a brief video and then use your participant journal to accomplish that week's challenge.

My name is Eric Ferris, creator and your host for *The Lent Experience*. I'm glad you've joined us!

Using TLE at Your Church

Will The Lent Experience *work at my church?*

The Lent Experience does not promote any specific church or denomination. We're confident that this resource is in the mainstream of the historic Christian faith and will be received well in any denomination.

Are there any copyright/broadcast restrictions?

Churches use *The Lent Experience* in a variety of ways. When you purchase journals for your participants it comes with free use of the videos. The videos on YouTube are set to be able to be embedded on your website, played during church services, or played at small group gatherings. We want as many people as possible to experience Lent, so feel free to use the videos however they work for your purposes. We do ask that if you post journal excerpts in any way or embed videos on your website that you include the following: *Used by permission from author — Eric Ferris*. We think it's great when churches create web pages, blogs, podcasts and other creative approaches to using *The Lent Experience*. Go for it! However, please

Using The Lent Experience at Your Church

remember that presenting someone else's material as your own is dishonest and digital redistribution of journal content is theft.

Is the content in this journal good for teaching a class?
No. *The Lent Experience* is not designed to be a class about Lent. It is designed for participants to experience Lent. The journals work in tandem with the videos to equip participants to engage in each week's challenge.

Is this a group experience or an individual experience?
Individual. What many churches or groups find helpful is that once it has been promoted and everyone has a journal, the experience pretty much runs itself. Many small groups and churches that use *The Lent Experience* gather to talk about their experience, but there are no group discussion guides that come with TLE.

Traditional?

Traditional?

Some people have asked how traditional my approach was going to be for this project. In other words, will this Lent Experience be the same as, let's say, those who observed

Lent 1,000 years ago?

My answer is yes and no. For the purists who don't like anything to be "messed with" this Lent Experience may not scratch their itch. I have several friends who are well educated in church history and spiritual formation. The truth is that I didn't create this with them in mind. My goal was much broader. The Lent Experience is designed to help people, both familiar and unfamiliar with liturgical calendar practices, to fully participate in Lent. I wanted to help those of us who grew up observing Lent ritualistically to discover the meaning and heart behind it and for those who grew up in evangelical churches or no church at all to discover how valuable it is to get in touch with some of these practices that Christians have observed for hundreds of years.

TRADITIONAL?

The Lent Experience is an attempt to embrace the heart and purpose of Lent traditions. I wanted to take the main elements of Lent and encourage people to experience them in their real lives in our current world. So, yes. The main elements of The Lent Experience have been practiced for hundreds of years. And, no. It's not exactly the same because I don't think we are the same and neither is our world.

I'm not sure I'd argue that what this project has become is the "best" way to observe Lent. I am a simple guy. If you encounter the Jesus that changed my life both now and for eternity then I will call that a win.

LENT FAQS

*How did Lent start?**

Originally Good Friday and Easter Day were observed as a single festival of the crucifixion and resurrection. From very early times this probably included a fast which was kept before the celebration. If you trace it back as far as you can go, you can find evidence that the Church, as early as AD 200, observed a season of preparation for Easter. In the following few centuries it also evolved into a season of instruction for new Christians to be baptized on Easter. The idea of fasting as a form of preparation for Easter comes from Jesus' statement that "The days will come when the bridegroom will be taken away from them, and then they will fast in that day" (Mark 2:20 ESV). How they observed the fast and how many days varied from church to church. The Church of Jerusalem was perhaps the first to observe a "Lenten" fast of forty days as early as the fourth century. How Lent has been observed has morphed throughout church history. Different branches of Christianity have observed Lent differently. However, what has remained mostly consistent is that Lent is a season of preparation for Easter that involves repentance (sorrowful reflection of our sinfulness), fasting/self-denial (to remind us we are dependent upon God), and almsgiving (to refocus on care and compassion for others).

What does the word "Lent" mean?

The word lent derives from the Anglo-Saxon (German) word for "spring". In describing the season before Easter, it eventually replaced the Latin word quadragesima which means "forty days". This occurred in the AD 1300's when local languages began to be used more and more in the church instead of Latin.

ABOUT LENT

Why are there so many versions of the liturgical calendar? Kudos to you if you know what a liturgical calendar is to even ask this question! The fast answer is that liturgical calendars are man-made tools to help us remember different things about Jesus in various seasons of the year. Each day or season of the liturgical calendar is meant to help us focus. Here are some basics you'll find in most liturgical calendars:

Advent—The four Sundays leading up to Christmas. Anticipation and preparation for the birth of Jesus. Some traditions use advent wreaths with candles to focus on a different aspect of His coming each week.

Christmas Day—A celebration of the incarnation of the Son of God.

Epiphany—This day (and season) focuses on the life of Jesus. The day is celebrated on January 6 and commemorates the visit of the magi to see Jesus. The season of Epiphany is situated between Christmas and Lent.

Ash Wednesday—This is the first day of Lent. The day focuses on repentance and humility before God.

Lent—The season of 40 days leading up to Easter (not counting the Sundays) that focuses on preparation for the crucifixion and resurrection.

Holy Week—This is often how people refer to the final week of Lent. It includes Palm Sunday (Jesus' triumphal entry into Jerusalem), Maundy Thursday (The Last Supper and Jesus Praying in the Garden), Good Friday (crucifixion), and Easter Sunday (resurrection). Good Friday, Holy Saturday, and Easter Sunday are sometimes referred to collectively as The Great Triduum.

Ascension Day—Forty days after Easter. This day commemorates Jesus' ascension to the right hand of the Father after his resurrection. The focus of this day is that Jesus is the rightful Lord (King) of all.

Pentecost—Seven weeks after Easter. This day commemorates the coming of the promised Holy Spirit.

Ordinary Time—If you Google "liturgical calendars", you will see this term. It's simply all of the days that are not special days or seasons.

Why is Lent 40 days?

Forty is a common number of days for preparation in Scripture. For example: Moses spent forty days on Mount Sinai receiving the covenant (10 commandments) from God. It rained for forty days and nights when Noah was on the ark (although he spent over a year on that thing). Jonah gave the people of Nineveh forty days to repent. Jesus spent forty days in the wilderness fasting when he was tempted by Satan. There's nothing magical about the number forty. It just makes some sense to use it for something preparatory like Lent.

What is Ash Wednesday and what's on their foreheads?

Ash Wednesday is the first day of Lent. Ash Wednesday church services are normally designed to help us focus on the realities of our own mortality, our sinful human state, and our need for Jesus for forgiveness and eternal life. In the Catholic Church (as well as some others) the ashes are made from burning the palm branches that were used in the Palm Sunday services the prior year. The placing of the ashes on the forehead using the thumb is normally done in the sign of the cross. Putting the ashes on the forehead is a reminder that "we came from the dust, and

ABOUT LENT

to the dust we will return". We are God's creation and we will one day die. The sign of the cross reminds us that eternal life is found only through the cross of Jesus. Many Christians leave the ashes on their foreheads all day as a sign of humility before God.

Why does Lent seem to be primarily a Catholic thing?
Simple answer? Because Catholics are the ones who observe Lent the most. Why? That's not such a simple answer. To answer it fully requires a lesson in church history. However, you can get a taste for the answer in the last question in this article.

What are you "giving up for Lent"?
Have you ever had someone ask you that question? Abstinence (giving up something good) and fasting (normally food) is a big part of Lent. Many people who observe Lent do two things. First, they give up something they take pleasure in for the entire season of Lent. Second, they fast certain foods or certain meals on certain days during Lent. We'll explore this more during *The Lent Experience*. However, reducing Lent to just "giving something up" as an act of willpower misses the point. Fasting is a very helpful spiritual discipline. It is definitely included in The Lent Experience, but it's part of the larger whole.

What's up with only eating fish on Fridays?
It's partly related to the answer to the previous question. Not eating meat (which fish is not

considered) on certain days during Lent is a very "Catholic" thing. What days a person is supposed to abstain from meat during Lent has changed throughout the years. How the whole "abstain from meat" idea developed over the centuries is an interesting topic, but requires way too long an explanation for these FAQ's.

Why do some people have a problem with Lent?
There's actually a pretty good reason. It is very possible that the purpose of Lent can be dangerously confused. If we fall into the trap of thinking that it is the good or religious things that we do that make us "OK" with God, then we seriously miss the point. There is nothing we can do to earn God's mercy or love. You don't earn mercy or love. You just accept it. In other words, no matter how hard we try to be "good" people, that effort falls very short. It is Jesus' death and resurrection that make a relationship with God possible. You could observe 1,000 Lents and it won't ever accomplish in your life what the cross of Jesus has. The Church Reformation of the 1600's led by Martin Luther was all about this topic. This was the big moment in history when we ended up with the Catholic / Protestant church split. The purpose of Lent is not ritual, good works, and earning favor with God. The purpose of Lent is to focus on why the death and resurrection of Jesus is so important. The observation of Lent is a choice, not an obligation.

*In addition to other resources, I found lots of good info for these FAQ's in- The Christian Calendar. L.W. Cowie & John Selwyn Gummer. G&C Merriam Company, Springfield, Mass, 1974.

VIDEOS

Finding *The Lent Experience* Videos

The Lent Experience project began in 2013 and has been revised several times over the years. Therefore, you might stumble upon some random, older videos and podcasts floating around out there online. To find the most up-to-date videos, you'll want to search *"The Lent Experience"* on either RightNow Media or YouTube.

The official videos for *The Lent Experience* appear in ONLY two places:

On RightNow Media

& YouTube.

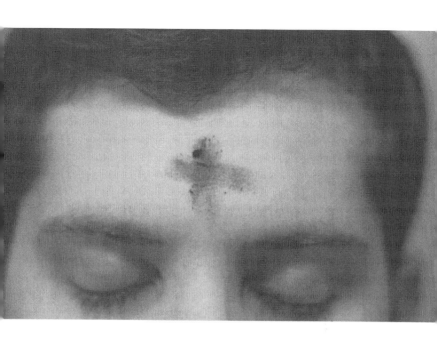

Getting ready to start!
Ash Wednesday

ASH WEDNESDAY

▶ Watch the video on Ash Wednesday and your Lent Experience will have begun.

Ash Wednesday is the first day of Lent. The date changes every year, so make sure you know when Ash Wednesday is this year.

Ash Wednesday prayer:
Take 5 minutes and write answers to these two questions:

 What you are thinking as you begin the Lent Experience?

 What are you hoping to get out of it?

Write it as a prayer to begin your experience.

GETTING READY TO START! ASH WEDNESDAY

Thoughts. Feelings. Prayers.

The Lent Experience Journal

GETTING READY TO START! ASH WEDNESDAY

The Lent Experience Journal

Challenge #1: Fasting

CHALLENGE #1: FASTING

 Watch the video for the first Sunday of Lent.

Here are a few thoughts on fasting for Lent that I hope will help you complete your week #1 challenge. Several of the ideas provided here (and much more) can be found in the book *Spiritual Disciplines for the Christian Life* by Donald Whitney (NavPress), which I highly recommend.

Is fasting something normal Christians do?

Let's start by acknowledging that Jesus seemed to think fasting would be something we would incorporate into our lives. The teachings of Jesus found in Matthew 6 include: meeting the needs of the poor, prayer, forgiving others, proper handling of wealth, trust in and loyalty to God, and fasting. I'm pretty sure very few of us would be willing to call any of these things unimportant. Well, except fasting. Why is fasting so broadly ignored as a normal part of the Christian life?

You will need to trust that I'm a normal guy when I say what I'm about to say. If you asked me to list the top five things that help me stay focused on God, useful for His purposes, and living in a God honoring way I would place regular fasting in that list. Yes, I fast regularly. I don't think that makes me "super-spiritual". In fact, it reminds me of the exact opposite. Without God at work in my life I am not a very good person. I'm prone to selfishness, anger and pride. I can be quick to speak and slow to listen. Very few things in my life combat this better than fasting.

What are the benefits of fasting?

There are many reasons to fast and there are several

CHALLENGE #1: FASTING

spiritual benefits. Here are three benefits of fasting that are worth considering specifically during *The Lent Experience*:

1. Fasting trains us to say no to our flesh—doesn't Mardi Gras make you wonder? Fat Tuesday is the day before Ash Wednesday and is designed to help people get all of their sin out of their system before entering the season of Lent. That certainly is an exercise in missing the point. On a very basic level, if we can say no to food when we are hungry then we are learning to take control over our bodies. So we say no to something that is good (like food) so that we learn how to say no to the temptation of sin. Fasting trains us how to say "no" to the flesh and "yes" to God (see Galatians 5).

2. Fasting reminds us of our weakness – It's amazing what effect skipping one meal can have on us. We are dependent creatures. In other words, we need things outside of ourselves to survive (like food and water). God is not like us. He is independent. He needs nothing outside of Himself to exist. When we are hungry and our stomachs are growling, it is a very tangible reminder that there is a God and we are not Him. It humbles us. It causes us to think rightly about ourselves. There are very few practical things you can do that teach this lesson more quickly than fasting.

3. Fasting increases our focus– There is no inherent spiritual value in skipping meals. We don't earn brownie points (please excuse the food reference) with God by fasting. When we fast for a reason, the fast helps us focus on that reason.

Being hungry constantly reminds us of what caused us to initiate the fast in the first place. In the case of The Lent Experience, our goal is to focus on the death and resurrection of Jesus. Here are some Scriptures that I would encourage you to read (perhaps several times) at some point during your fast. (Colossians 2:6-3:17; Ephesians 2)

What Fasting is Not
- Fasting is not just a short season of obedience to God. I always find it funny when people give up really bad things for Lent. It's like saying, "Ok God, just for this few weeks I'm gonna be good".

- Fasting is not a trick. Many people who feel obligated to fast during Lent will choose to "give up" things that they don't like anyway. Sorry, that doesn't fool God.

- Fasting is not a spiritual temper tantrum. It's not a way to force God to do what we want Him to do. "I prayed. God didn't answer. I'll force God to answer by fasting and praying." It just doesn't work that way.

Tips for Fasting
- There may be some medical reasons that you would want to consult your doctor before fasting. If you have any question about how fasting will affect you medically, please contact a physician.

- Abstaining from food is the primary way people fast and is specifically this week's challenge. However, people also initiate fasts that abstain from things like social media, TV, or sex.

CHALLENGE #1: FASTING

- When breaking your fast, don't pig out. You'll regret it. Your first meal after any length of fasting should be healthy and light. This will take self-control since you'll be hungry.

- Drink water.

- Expect to not feel great. You may get a headache. Taking medicine is not a violation of your fast.

The Lent Experience Journal

Thoughts. Feelings. Prayers.

CHALLENGE #1: FASTING

The Lent Experience Journal

CHALLENGE #1: FASTING

The Lent Experience Journal

Challenge 2: Silence & Solitude

CHALLENGE #2: SOLITUDE

 Watch the video for the second Sunday of Lent.

Why solitude?
Why solitude? Because listening to a radio station and a Barbie movie while driving is annoying. What? This makes sense. I promise.

We used to have a portable television that we put in the minivan on long trips so the kids could watch movies. The TV was somewhat old-school. Therefore, the sound for the television was sent over a selected radio station so that it would come through the van's speakers. Sometimes it worked well: the sound for the movie was crystal clear and the only thing you would hear. Other times you'd get a maddening mix of the actual radio station and the television sound. When that happened, you couldn't really hear either. Too much noise! Frustrating! Exactly!

The Benefits of Solitude
Ever wonder why Jesus seemed to have a laser-focused awareness on what the Father wanted Him to do in any given moment? Ever wonder why Jesus had such a clear sense of the purpose and mission for His life? Before you just chalk it up the fact that Jesus was God in human form, take a look at these verses: Matthew 4:1, Matthew 14:23, Mark 1:35, and Luke 4:42. Jesus took time to get away to just be with the Father.

We should do the same. Perhaps the reason many of us struggle so much when it comes to hearing the voice of God, knowing the Father's will and being strong enough to do those things we know we ought to do, is that we

CHALLENGE #2: SILENCE & SOLITUDE

spend so very little time alone with our heavenly Father.

Solitude is the only way to tune out all of the noise of life. If I truly want to know God and learn to hear His voice, I must get rid of all of the noise clutter. Now does my van analogy make sense?

The biggest benefit of solitude is that it is there that you cultivate communication with your heavenly Father. In solitude we find restoration, refreshment, strength, and focus. Are you lacking in those things?

Tips for Your Hour of Silence & Solitude

I'm going to resist the urge to "over-program" your time. These tips are meant to at least give you some ideas to get started.

- Don't turn it into reading time. There's a big difference between spending an hour of solitude in thinking/prayer and curling up with a good book. Reading is great…it's just not the point of this kind of solitude.

- Bring your journal. Write down thoughts and prayers.

- Be honest. Talk to God. He can handle your honesty (and your tears, and your frustrations, and your questions, and your silence, and… OK, you get it). I'm sure you already know this, but talking to God doesn't have to be audible.

- Four things to think about (maybe take 5 minutes each to think and write):

- I'm a mover. Feel free to find a good trail and go for a walk. When it's cold, I drive around in my car. (But then

I see people and have to pay attention to driving...more distraction. Maybe there's a secluded place to park?)

- Listen! There's nothing you can tell God He doesn't already know. There's a lot God could tell you that you have no clue about.

- It will be tough if you're too comfortable. A fluffy couch in front of the fireplace is a bad idea.

- You may feel like you're wasting time. That's expected and actually part of our problem.

 God.

 You.

 Sin.

 The Cross.

CHALLENGE #2: SILENCE & SOLITUDE

Thoughts. Feelings. Prayers.

The Lent Experience Journal

CHALLENGE #2: SILENCE & SOLITUDE

The Lent Experience Journal

Challenge 3: Repentance

CHALLENGE #3: REPENTANCE

 Watch the video for the third Sunday of Lent.

The challenge this week is to set aside 30 minutes to engage in the discipline of repentance. For some reason the word "repent" carries some negative baggage with it. I've got a few hunches as to why, but to keep this short I'll keep my opinions to myself. What I'm hoping for this week is that we all gain a new appreciation for what a gift from God and opportunity repentance really is!

CONFESSION = ACKNOWLEDGMENT/AGREEMENT

REPENTANCE = TO THINK DIFFERENTLY

There's a slight difference between confession and repentance. However, the two work really well together. We read about confession in 1 John together in this week's video. Confession is about acknowledgment and agreement. How great is God?! He says if we'll just acknowledge our sin and agree with Him about it that He'll forgive us and cleanse us from it! How good is that?!

Repentance goes a little further. We find repentance talked about a lot in the Gospels and in Acts. Repentance is to think differently about something. A change in how we think about something which then causes us to act differently. In the Gospels and in Acts, we are invited to think differently about how we are living our lives.

Set aside a 30 minute block of time. Pick your day, time and location. Then...

CHALLENGE #3: REPENTANCE

1. Ask God, in your own words, to shine His light into your life and help you to see things for what they really are.

2. Use the following Scriptures to take inventory about the sin in your life. Read slowly, think, and trust that God is answering the prayer you just prayed in Step 1. Jot down thoughts as you go. These lists aren't every possible sin, but they will prompt you to think well about your life.

The Ten Commandments—Exodus 20:1-17
Holy Spirit vs Sinful Nature—Galatians 5:16-26
Am I A Loving Person?—1 Corinthians 13

3. Confess. You've got all kinds of thoughts right now after praying and reading these Scriptures. Are you willing to be honest with God? Will you acknowledge and agree with God? Talk to Him about that.

4. Repent. Are you willing to make the choice to think and act differently? Think about that and talk to Him about it. Write some things down.

That's all. It's that simple!

Repentance is a great gift! God loves you. If you feel at all beat up after this exercise, that's the enemy. Satan is a liar. He condemns us and tells us lies like we are unlovable, or unforgivable, or hopeless. God loves you. Forgives you. Cleanses you. Accepts you. He helps you hit the reset button. Receive that today!

THE LENT EXPERIENCE JOURNAL

Thoughts. Feelings. Prayers.

CHALLENGE #3: REPENTANCE

The Lent Experience Journal

CHALLENGE #3: REPENTANCE

The Lent Experience Journal

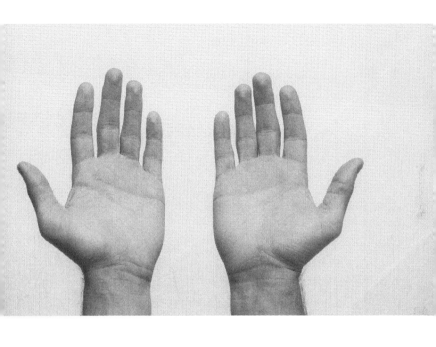

Challenge 4: Almsgiving

CHALLENGE #4: ALMSGIVING

 Watch the video for the fourth Sunday of Lent.

Alms. It's a word that's not used much anymore. We're not sure what it is, much less how we would give it! The word comes to us in English through a few languages. At the heart of the meaning of this word are compassion and mercy. Almsgiving is an act of love by which we meet someone else's practical needs.

Our hearts are beating more in rhythm with the heartbeat of God when we are actively and sacrificially giving to meet the needs of others. I need this reminder regularly because I live in an affluent, suburban area. It would be a great act of self-deception to think that I am not affected by the selfishness, self-absorption, materialism, excessive consumption, and selfish ambition of the area in which I live. It's all around me and I fear it has a greater effect on me than I may even realize. It's an honest assessment to ask this question: Am I becoming more like Jesus or more like the culture in which I live?

God has always been concerned for the weak, the needy, the marginalized, and the defenseless. Furthermore, He is concerned that we are concerned as well.

Leave some for Others
When God established his covenant with the people of Israel at Mt. Sinai, he communicated with great clarity what was expected of His people. While these stipulations (laws) seem stale to many, they actually reveal much about the heart of God and what He values.

CHALLENGE #4: ALMSGIVING

Leviticus 19:9-10 NIV

> *"'When you reap the harvest of your land, do not reap to the very edges of your field or gather the gleanings of your harvest. Do not go over your vineyard a second time or pick up the grapes that have fallen. Leave them for the poor and the alien. I am the Lord your God."*

No...we don't get a pass because the vast majority of us are not farmers. The idea here is that the people of God should care about one another by caring about the needs of others. Did you notice that this included "aliens" too? This challenges us to care for those outside of our normal relational sphere. This should show up in our lives in very practical ways. God expected and still does expect His people to limit their own consumption in order to provide for the needs of others.

Avoid Religious Charades
James 1:27

> *"Religion that God our Father accepts as pure and faultless is this: to look after orphans and widows in their distress and to keep oneself from being polluted by the world."* NIV

God has never really been ambiguous about what He thinks about us going through the motions of religion. He's not much impressed by our singing on Sunday if our lives sing the song of selfishness the rest of the week.

Understanding "true religion" is as much a heart issue as it is an intellectual issue. God loves people. God cares about how people are treated. God cares about how we treat people to the extent that it seems to be at the very heart of how he evaluates how genuine our faith in Him really is. It's like He's saying "You love me? Good. Then love them." This makes me uncomfortable because I'm not so sure I would give myself high marks with this. So what do I do?

To be clear, we don't earn our salvation and entrance into the eternal kingdom by doing kind things. Nor does this mean that God is saying that our gatherings to worship and hear His Word taught are not important. It is, however, clear in Scripture that we demonstrate our faith in and loyalty to God by living it out in our homes, our churches, our business offices, our schools, and our communities. True religion and genuine faith is evidenced by living a life that increasingly includes acts of mercy, justice, and giving oneself for orphans, the poor, the widow, the struggling single mom, the fatherless kid, the prisoner, the sick, etc.

Here are a few more references for you to consider: Isaiah 58, Matthew 6:1-4, Matthew 22:34-40, Matthew 25, Gal 2:10.

Three ideas for this week. Pick one and go for it!

Keep your eyes open. Simply ask God "Who do you want me to help and what do you want me to do?" Then go throughout your normal day looking for the answer. You'll likely be surprised at how much more you notice all around you.

Explore donating to your local church or a local organization that meets the needs of people. This could be time, money, food, giving things you already own, buying new things, etc. You may be surprised at what you learn about what's

CHALLENGE #4: ALMSGIVING

going on in your community or things your church does of which you were not aware.

3 That idea or person that's in your head right now. You've thought about it, but maybe have put it off or haven't been sure exactly what to do. Do it...this week...even if you do it imperfectly.

Thoughts. Feelings. Prayers.

The Lent Experience Journal

CHALLENGE #4: ALMSGIVING

The Lent Experience Journal

CHALLENGE #4: ALMSGIVING

The Lent Experience Journal

Challenge 5: Forgiveness

CHALLENGE #5: FORGIVENESS

 Watch the video for the fifth Sunday of Lent.

I hesitantly write this because I know that this topic requires much more than a brief article. This article is my attempt to provide enough information and motivation for participants to effectively engage with this week's challenge.

I've learned over the years to forgive *immediately*. Keeping short accounts is a much better way to live. Therefore, this week's challenge is pretty easy for me. I know that is not true for everyone.

This week's challenge might be as simple as a good refresher for you OR it may cut to the heart of unresolved issues in your life and require the best you've got and then some. Either way...I'm praying for you this week. Forgiveness is a core issue in the life of the every believer. Think of forgiveness as the key that unlocks the door to freedom.

I Need Forgiveness

This world is a messed up place. That's pretty easy to recognize. What's the problem? I'm not talking about a list of symptoms. I'm asking about the root cause. What makes this world so messed up? God diagnoses it as a sin problem. Each one of us has an internal "sin" problem. The world is messed up because we are messed up. Wanna change the world? Start with you. There are so many ways that we ignore, offend, rebel against, speak badly about, mistrust, and disobey our Creator God. Jesus endured the punishment that all of that deserves. We, in exchange, are

CHALLENGE #5: FORGIVENESS

offered forgiveness and reconciliation with God.

Read Matthew 6:12 and 1 John 1:8-10.

Need to Forgive Those Who Have Sinned Against Me

Once we recognize God to be forgiving, patient, and gracious it requires something of us. We are supposed to extend that same grace to others.

Read Matthew 6:12-15, Luke 6:27-36 and Matthew 18:21-35.

Your sin has affected other people. And other people's sin has affected you. It's a reality of the world we live in. We can clamor for fairness. And on one level we'd be right. It wasn't fair. One person suffering from the sin of another isn't fair. One day Jesus is going to return to set up his eternal kingdom. When He does, He will put an end to all sin, evil and suffering. But right now we live in a world marred by sin. Forgiveness is the only way to navigate such a world in a healthy way.

If someone has done something and you are still carrying anger, bitterness, resentment or some other negative and destructive emotion, then you need to know that forgiveness is the way to freedom. You don't necessarily need to talk to the person who sinned against you to forgive them. You need to talk to God about it. The emotions attached to these issues are real. This kind of praying is gritty, honest, emotional, and tough. Forgiveness is a choice, not a feeling. Your feelings are real, but if you wait to forgive until you "feel like it" — it may never happen. You can choose to obey God and forgive today. Some day your feelings might catch up with your choice.

Take some time in your journal. You'll need to make a list. Your list might be very short or longer than you anticipated. Each instance might be a small thing or a big thing. For each instance write: What happened? How did it make you feel? Then talk to God about your choice to forgive.

The Steps to Freedom in Christ by Neil Andersen (Harvest House Publishers) is as helpful a summary of how to actively engage in forgiveness as I've ever seen. If this week's challenge is particularly difficult for you, I would encourage you to visit www.ficm.org. There is a free download called *Forgiving Others* that may help you with this week's challenge. You may also want to pick up a copy of the book *Steps to Freedom in Christ* or *The Bondage Breaker*.

I Need to Reconcile with Those I Have Sinned Against
Read Matthew 5:23-26.

If you've wronged someone and have never apologized and attempted to restore the relationship, then this week is your week! The longer you wait, the less likely you are to do it! There's no guarantee as to how the person will respond to you. They may forgive you. They may not. You may become friends again. You may not. Their response is not the point. The point is that we, as Christ followers, are obedient to God.

CHALLENGE #5: FORGIVENESS

Thoughts. Feelings. Prayers.

The Lent Experience Journal

CHALLENGE #5: FORGIVENESS

The Lent Experience Journal

Challenge 6: Bible Reading

CHALLENGE #6: BIBLE READING

 Watch the video for the sixth Sunday of Lent.

There are four Gospels. Each Gospel is about the life, death, and resurrection of Jesus. Each Gospel writer puts together their account in a way that emphasizes certain things about Jesus. So while each Gospel is noticeably different in how it reads, all four Gospels share an emphasis on the final week of Jesus' life, the crucifixion, and resurrection.

Therefore, I could have chosen from any of the four Gospels for our Holy Week reading challenge. Below is a reading schedule from the Gospel of Luke. If you'd like to read from the others Gospels, I've also noted where the final week of Jesus' life picks up in each of the other three Gospels.

Holy Week Reading Schedule
- Monday- Luke 19:28-48
- Tuesday- Luke 20
- Wednesday- Luke 21
- Thursday- Luke 22
- Friday- Luke 23
- Saturday- Luke 24

Note: The Passion of Jesus (His final week) can also be read starting in these places: Matthew 21, Mark 11, and John 12.

CHALLENGE #6: BIBLE READING

Thoughts. Feelings. Prayers.

The Lent Experience Journal

CHALLENGE #6: BIBLE READING

THE LENT EXPERIENCE JOURNAL

Wrapping it all up

WRAPPING IT ALL UP—AFTER EASTER REFLECTION

You made it! Way to go! Here are a few questions to think about and write about.

1. Was Easter celebration any different for you after engaging in *The Lent Experience*? If so, what was different?

2. Look back at your Ash Wednesday journal entry. How did God answer your prayer?

3. Were there any "a-ha!" moments for you during *The Lent Experience*? What were they?

4. What was ONE main takeaway from *The Lent Experience* that will change the way you do things going forward?

WRAPPING IT ALL UP—AFTER EASTER REFLECTION

Thoughts. Feelings. Prayers.

THE LENT EXPERIENCE JOURNAL

WRAPPING IT ALL UP—AFTER EASTER REFLECTION

The Lent Experience Journal

WRAPPING IT ALL UP—AFTER EASTER REFLECTION

About the Author

Ferris wheels are fun. Simple. Not complicated. A delightfully diverse group of people constantly embarking and disembarking. Some perhaps a bit apprehensive of new heights, but everyone enjoying the ride and taking in the surrounding views from a new perspective.

Eric Ferris enjoys inviting people to "ride the ferris wheel" of the local church. He's spent his entire adult life captivated by and serving in local Christian churches. Why? That's simple too. Jesus loves His Church. Jesus died for His Church. Jesus is building His Church. And one day Jesus is coming back for His Church. For Eric, to genuinely follow Jesus is to choose to love the thing that Jesus loves the most.

Eric Ferris currently serves at Christ Community Church (ccclife.org) in the western suburbs of Chicago. Having served at several influential churches in the USA, Eric is known for his love for the local church, bringing clarity in complexity, and a straightforward approach to life and ministry. Eric and his wife, D'Ann, have four children– Michael, Courtney, Erin and Katie.

WRAPPING IT ALL UP—AFTER EASTER REFLECTION

Contact

Eric stays pretty busy pastoring in his local church, but if he might be able to help you and the mission of your church, hit 'em up! From guest speaking to Zoom visits for groups using *The Lent Experience*, he'd be happy to be an encouragement. Who knows, he may even share his Jelly Belly® jelly beans with you or let you challenge him to a game of ping pong. Simply visit ccclife.org.

Made in the USA
Columbia, SC
22 March 2025